The Art of Freelance Writing

Build a Profitable Writing Business

Table of Contents

Chapter 1. Introduction

Immerse yourself in the transformative world of freelance writing! This Special Report, titled 'The Art of Freelance Writing: Build a Profitable Writing Business,' is what you need to shift gears and accelerate your journey from obscurity into the remarkable universe of freelance writing. In this illuminating piece, you'll discover the expert-tested secrets, strategies, and resources that can propel your freelance writing passion into a thriving, fruitful venture. It's time to uncover the power of words, embrace independence, and command the rewards you deserve! This Special Report is your joyous ticket to creative autonomy and financial independence, guaranteed to spur you into the exciting realm of freelance writing. Buy it today, and let your journey towards a profitable writing business begin!

Chapter 2. Understanding the Freelance Writing Landscape

Freelance writing can be a rewarding and fruitful profession with an enticing sense of creative liberty and income potential. But as with any industry, it's vital to navigate the landscape with a keen understanding of its highs, lows, opportunities, and challenges. Let's embark on a journey that would help you understand this landscape more comprehensively.

2.1. Knowing Your Niche

To begin with, it's essential to identify and define the area in which you want to specialize - your niche. Your niche is a specific segment in the freelance writing market that fits your expertise, passion, and the demand of the market. It could be blogging, copywriting, technical writing, academic writing, journalistic writing, and so on.

Given the expansive universe of writing, narrowing down your focus is crucial to leverage your skills and knowledge. Discover your area of interest, ensure there's a market for it, and begin honing your skills for this specific niche.

2.2. The Different Types of Writing Jobs

Freelance writing envelops numerous channels. Skill sets and expertise required can vary significantly from one job type to another. Here are few prominent freelance writing jobs to consider:

1. Blogging: This is both informal and personalised, targeting a specific audience group.

2. Copywriting: This involves promotional and advertising writing, including website content, brochures, emails, and more.

3. Technical Writing: This involves creating instruction manuals, FAQs, product descriptions, and more.

4. Content Writing: This is a broad category involving writing digital content for websites, social media, and more.

5. Journalistic Writing: This involves news articles, investigative stories, and feature articles.

Knowing the job types would determine which clients to pursue and what skills to hone.

2.3. The Role of Market Research

A firm understanding of the freelance writing market is another essential part of the landscape. Delve into research that can provide insights on the demand for various niches, prevailing rates, competition, and the most lucrative sectors. Market research would also uncover the upcoming trends and sectors that are rapidly growing, offering new windows of opportunity.

2.4. Understanding Rates and Compensation

Navigating the financial elements of freelance writing is crucial. Usually, rates vary across different writing styles, project complexities, client types, and experience levels. Typically, there are three essential ways freelancers charge - per word, per hour, or per project.

For per word rates, you charge a specific rate for every word you write. For hourly rates, you estimate the number of hours you would require to complete a project and charge accordingly. For project-based rates, you assess the scope of the project as a whole and charge a flat fee.

Also crucial to note is the importance of having a contract in place that clearly outlines your rate, scope of work, payment terms, rights to the content, revision policies, and more.

2.5. The Importance of Networking

Freelance writing is not just about writing but also about being a part of a community. Networking is an essential part of this landscape. Associating with writers' communities, attending seminars, engaging in social media communities, and nurturing relationships with industry influencers can open doors to more opportunities. It's also beneficial to connect with clients, editors, and other industry professionals who could provide valuable advice and potential job leads.

2.6. Building a Portfolio

For a freelance writer, your portfolio is your resume. It showcases your writing prowess and variety to potential clients. A compelling portfolio should house a diverse range of your best works. Ensure to include pieces that align with your niche and the job you are targeting.

2.7. Embracing the Learning Curve

Freelance writing is a dynamic and evolving field. To stay competitive, embrace the perennial process of learning, upskilling, and adapting to the market's changing needs. Dominate new writing styles, learn about trending topics, grow your knowledge in your niche, and keep refining your skills.

In sum, understanding the freelance writing landscape paves the way for a successful venture. It equips you with the knowledge and tools needed to navigate the market, allowing you to carve your unique space and thrive.

Chapter 3. Identifying Your Specialized Niche

The first major step to becoming a successful freelance writer is finding your specialized niche. You may have a knack for words in general, but honing your skills and focusing your efforts on a particular area can make your journey more fruitful. Dive in as we explore how to identify your specialized niche in freelance writing.

3.1. The Importance of a Niche

You'll find many reasons why highlighting a specialized niche is integral to your freelance writing career. By focusing on a specific niche, you can work towards becoming an expert in that field, increasing your reputation and ultimately attracting higher-paying clients who are looking for specialized knowledge. A niche can help differentiate you from the myriad of writers out there,

Chapter 4. Building a Striking Portfolio

Understanding the significance of a portfolio to a freelance writer is the first step to creating one that stands out from the crowd. Whether it's your first foray into freelance writing or you're an experienced freelancer plotting your next move, an engaging, diverse, and powerful portfolio is pivotal. It's not merely a collection of your best pieces; it's a visual representation of what you bring to the table, illustrating your writing style, range, and skills to potential clients.

4.1. What to Include in Your Portfolio

When compiling a portfolio that will attract the attention and admiration of clients, you should select your work samples carefully. You want to display your prowess while also demonstrating the diversity or specialization of your writing skills. Here are the essential elements that should constitute your portfolio:

- Articles, blog posts, or short stories that reflect your writing style and skills

- Snippets from larger works such as books or extensive research papers

- Guest posts written for other publications

- Testimonials from previous clients or colleagues

- Awards or recognitions you've achieved

Remember that your portfolio, just like you as a freelancer, is a work in progress. It should grow and evolve as you do, capturing your progress and reflecting changes in your style or focus.

4.2. Achieving Diversity in Your Portfolios

Here's an aspect more subtle but of equal importance: the diverseness of your portfolio. If you specialize in a particular type of writing, showcasing various tones, formats, and styles within that niche can show off your dynamism and adaptability. If you're a versatile writer who can cover various topics, your portfolio should reflect that range.

Let's view two scenarios to drive this point home:

1. If you primarily write blog pieces for the health and wellness industry, that doesn't mean all your pieces should sound alike. Show different facets of your voice – showcase serious analytical pieces, informative guides, and perhaps a personal experience story.

2. As a generalist, you might pen articles across vastly different domains – from technology to travel. In this case, your portfolio should demonstrate your ability to adapt your tone and language as per the topic's requirement, signaling your diverse writing capabilities.

This array in your portfolio indicates to potential clients that you can handle a wide range of assignments, thereby widening your market.

4.3. Choosing Quality over Quantity

While it's vital to display diversity, don't be tempted to stuff your portfolio with everything you've ever written. Be selective with the work you display. The goal here is to showcase your best pieces to impress your audience. Therefore, prioritize quality over quantity.

If you're just starting out and don't have many pieces to choose from, that's alright. Focus on creating a few high-quality pieces for your portfolio rather than a slew of mediocre ones.

4.4. Crafting Engaging Portfolio Descriptions

Each piece in your portfolio is a story, but it's the accompanying descriptions that provide context to that story. These descriptions should effectively communicate the piece's purpose, highlighting the subject matter, any specific challenges overcome, and the piece's impact, if possible.

Say, for instance, you include an ebook you wrote for a tech start-up in your portfolio. Your description might read, "This comprehensive eBook aimed at explaining 'Blockchain Technology' was targeted at non-technical startup founders. Faced with the challenge of simplifying highly technical information, I developed engaging analogies, eventually leading to a 20% increase in the client's user base."

Such descriptions not only outline the scope of your work but also indicate your understanding of target audiences, thereby showcasing your prowess as a writer.

4.5. Showcasing Testimonials and Reviews

One powerful way to establish credibility and foster trust in your portfolio is to include testimonials from satisfied clients. Testimonials build social proof, making potential clients more comfortable in hiring you.

In each testimonial, aim to highlight the project's scope, your role in its success, and any specific qualities or skills that aided you in executing the task. Ultimately, each testimonial should paint a picture of your competence and reliability. If possible, ask for a picture or a logo from the client, as visuals tend to make testimonials look more authentic and compelling.

4.6. Regularly Updating Your Portfolio

Lastly, it's crucial to keep your portfolio up-to-date. Replace outdated work samples with fresh, relevant ones that align with your evolving skills. Also, remember to update your portfolio with any new testimonials, awards, and recognitions you receive.

Building a striking portfolio is not an overnight task, but a continuous process that goes hand in hand with your freelance writing journey. A dynamic, comprehensive, and evidence-backed portfolio is an essential tool in showcasing your skills, diversity, and reliability, thereby making it easier for you to land lucrative writing gigs.

Chapter 5. Pitching with Power: Winning Potential Clients

Writing effective pitches is the bridge that connects you, a freelance writer, to your prospective clients. It is the vital key that opens the door of opportunities and success in any freelance writing journey. This section of the report holds the comprehensive guide that can boost your pitching power and unlock the strategies to win potential clients.

5.1. Understanding Your Audience

Before reaching for your computer and typing away your pitch, the first and the most crucial step is to understand who you are writing for. Take the time to research your prospective client. Understand their industry, their brand voice, their mission, and vision. This understanding will help you tailor the message in your pitch to speak directly to your potential client's needs and expectations.

Make sure to demonstrate your knowledge about the client's business in the pitch. This can be done by mentioning a recent development or a specific product. That shows your dedication and the effort you have put in, and more often than not, it leaves a powerful impression.

5.2. Crafting the Perfect Pitch

Once you've got a firm grasp on who your prospective client is, the next step is to write the pitch. Your pitch should be concise, yet compelling. Begin with an engaging opening that grabs their attention immediately. It could be a provocative question or an intriguing statement.

The body of your pitch should carry the substance. It should contain relevant samples of your work, your related writing experiences, and how you can add value to their organization. Your samples shouldn't just be some random pieces of writing; they should match the tone and type of content the client produces.

Remember, the key is personalization. Avoid using generic statements. Address the recipient by their name and make the content of the pitch specific to their company. In a world where businesses receive countless pitches daily, standing out through personalization can give you an edge.

Towards the end of the pitch, place a strategic call-to-action. This provides an easy way for the client to take the next step, whether it's a request for an interview, to view your portfolio, or to make a decision.

5.3. Avoiding Common Pitfalls

There are some common pitfalls you need to avoid in creating your pitches:

1. Using a generic template: Avoid this at all costs. As mentioned earlier, personalization is paramount in successful pitches.
2. A failure to proofread: Typos scream unprofessionalism. Ensure your pitch is free of grammatical errors and typos.
3. Sounding desperate: Maintain a professional tone throughout. It's essential to show your enthusiasm but evade sounding desperate.

Always aim to strike a balance between showcasing your skills and painting a picture of how they fit into the client's requirements.

5.4. Following Up and Building Relationships

Following up on your pitch is equally important to crafting it. If you do not hear back, wait for a week or two, and then send a polite follow-up email. This demonstrates your genuine interest in the project.

But remember, there's a thin line between following up and spamming. Avoid crossing it. Send a maximum of two follow-up emails.

The world of freelance writing thrives on relationships. Build rapport with your clients. Meet deadlines, maintain open communication, and always be open to feedback. This will not only pave way for good reviews, but it can also lead to quality referrals.

So, remind yourself this — your pitch is not just a gateway to your next writing gig, it is a stepping stone towards building a long-lasting client relationship.

5.5. In Conclusion

Pitching with power is more than just writing a persuasive email to a prospective client. It's about understanding your audience, crafting messages that resonate with them, avoiding common mistakes, and staying consistent in your pursuit. It's about showcasing your skills and value in a way that compels your prospects to say yes.

With these strategies and principles, you can craft powerful pitches that will help you stand out in the market, win over potential clients, and start on this joyous venture towards creative autonomy and financial independence.

Remember, every 'no' is a step closer to your next 'yes'! Let this not be an intimidating process, but a journey of continuous learning and improvement. Now, take these expert-tested secrets and power up your pitching game!

Pitching with power is a matter of persistence, dedication, and patience. Arm yourself with these strategies, and you'll be on your way to a prosperous freelance writing career!

Chapter 6. Harnessing the Power of Networking

Freelance writing, for all its independence and opportunities for creative expression, is not a solitary profession. Networking is an essential aspect of building your business, both for generating client leads and to situate yourself within the writing community. Harnessing this networking auspiciously can make the difference between scraping by and experiencing a flourishing, profitable career.

6.1. Identify Your Network

Before you start reaching out to others, it's important to understand who is part of your potential network. Essentially, your network includes anyone who can provide support, insight, collaboration, or job opportunities.

This involves not just other writers and potential clients, but also editors, marketing professionals, web developers, graphic designers, and more. Harnessing a diverse network can facilitate access to various opportunities and resources. Remember, however, that networking is a two-way street. Think about what you can provide to your network as well, whether it's referrals, content, collaboration, or insight.

6.2. Where to Find Your Network

In this digital age, there are many places to find potential networking connections. This can range from industry conferences and local meetups, to online platforms like LinkedIn, Twitter, or industry-specific forums.

Forming part of relevant online communities such as social media groups, blog comment sections, and writing forums can be a valuable way to establish your presence. Ensure also to attend writing workshops, seminars, and book fairs. These platforms allow you to interact and share ideas with like-minded individuals and potential clients.

6.3. Leveraging Online Networking Tools

LinkedIn, as a professional networking tool, allows you to connect with other professionals, join groups pertinent to your industry, and provide a platform for your portfolio. In fact, it is not uncommon for potential employers to scout writers via LinkedIn, so maintaining an up-to-date, professional profile is essential.

Twitter may seem less professional, but it provides a perfect channel for engaging with others in your industry in a casual, conversational manner. With its emphasis on interaction and quick, concise messages, Twitter represents a vibrant, active community of writers that you can readily engage.

Freelance job platforms like Upwork, Freelancer, and Fiverr also offer excellent opportunities to build your network while directly engaging with potential clients.

6.4. Networking Etiquette

When building relationships, maintain a professional-level discourse and be courteous, respectful, articulate, and authentic. Do not be too pushy or make your only interaction about seeking job opportunities. Establishing relationships takes time and consistency, so be patient.

Additionally, make a point of expressing gratitude when others offer assistance or advice and, when possible, reciprocate. This not only displays good manners but also strengthens your professional relationship.

6.5. Maintain and Grow Your Network

Maintaining touch with individuals in your network is equally essential. Send emails to check in with contacts, comment on their articles or posts, offer assistance when required, and introduce them to others in your network when appropriate.

Never underestimate the value of a strong network in your success as a freelance writer. It opens up potential opportunities, provides a platform for collaboration, and offers a valuable resource of ideas and advice. By harnessing the power of networking, you can build a profitable, fulfilling writing business that takes full advantage of the community around you.

Just as your writing skills should continually grow and evolve, so should your network. Regularly attend industry events, join new professional groups, and keep an eye out for potential new contacts online or in-person. As you grow your freelance business, your network should grow alongside it, providing continuous opportunities for collaboration, personal growth, and client leads.

Remember, networking isn't just about business transactions; it's about forming lasting, genuine relationships in your industry. Don't underestimate the power of a friendly message, a shared interest, or a mutual connection. These simple interpersonal elements can be the foundation of a strong network and, in turn, a prosperous freelance business. In the world of freelance writing, your network is, without a doubt, one of your biggest assets.

Chapter 7. Smart Pricing: Valuing Your Work Right

Understanding the importance of accurate pricing can be the turning point in your freelance writing business. Once you fully comprehend how to price your work right and value what you offer, you set yourself on a path towards "smart pricing," which will substantially boost your profitability and ensure the longevity of your enterprise.

7.1. Setting the Right Price

The skill of setting the right price might seem abstract initially. It's like trying to hit a moving target in a dense fog. But rest assured, that fog will clear gradually as we explore the strategy of setting the right price.

To start with, it's crucial to dissociate your self-worth from the value of the work you produce. Yes, your writing is an art, honed and perfected over countless hours of practice and dedication. But, when it comes to pricing your work, it's best to view your work as a service where, like any other industry, supply influences demand and pricing.

The first step is researching what established freelance writers in your area of expertise charge for their work. The internet provides numerous platforms where you can find this information and gather data to establish a benchmark. Remember, comparing rates is not about under-valuing or over-pricing your work; it's about establishing a baseline.

7.2. Cost-Based Pricing

Traditional methods of determining the worth of a product or service usually come down to a straightforward calculation of costs versus desired profits. While some freelancers may undervalue their work and accept lower payments to compete based on cost, this is neither a sustainable nor a profitable long-term strategy.

When it comes to cost-based pricing, consider all aspects that eventually go into your work. These encompass both 'direct costs', like the time it takes to research, write, and edit the article, software subscriptions, and 'indirect costs' like utilities, marketing efforts, or even your workspace cost. Adding a margin for profits on top of that cost will give you a minimum base price. However, this doesn't mean that you'll sell your work at this price. It's the bottom-most price under which it would not be worth selling your work.

Bear in mind that this is a simplified way to calculate your time's worth. The true value often extends beyond mere costs and margins.

7.3. The Value-Based Pricing Approach

Value-based pricing is another popular pricing model, which involves charging clients based on the perceived value of your work. Unlike cost-based pricing, this approach requires a deeper understanding of the complexity of the project and the professional value you stand to deliver.

The key to successfully implementing this model is understanding the client's perspective. It involves being able to articulate the distinctive value you bring to the project, capture the level of expertise you provide, and, most importantly, justify your price with the benefits that your work will generate for the client.

Understanding their pain points, objectives, and intended outcome of the project will give you a clear idea of the value you're providing. This equips you to price your services higher, especially for projects that generate considerable revenue, recognition, or savings for the client.

7.4. Negotiating Prices

While initial pricing is crucial, so too is being a proficient negotiator. This skill is essential as clients often propose budget reductions or ask for an increased amount of work at the same price, affecting your bottom line.

Firstly, ensure your clients understand the detailed breakdown, rationale, and value behind your pricing - this will make negotiations easier. Additionally, have a pricing buffer that allows some room for negotiation and be fully prepared to walk away if the price dips lower than your established baseline. Remember, standing firm on your quality and prices sets a precedence for future projects with the same client, paving the way for a profitable long-term relationship.

7.5. Regular Review and Adjustment

Smart pricing is not a one-time task. It needs regular introspection, reassessment, and adjustment based on factors like market fluctuations, improved skills, expanded portfolio, inflation, and even currency exchange rates, among others.

Keep tracking your actual working hours per project and adjust your future prices accordingly. Improving your speed without compromising quality means you can deliver the same value in less time, leading to an indirect price increase that benefits you rather than the client.

In conclusion, pricing your freelance writing services is an art, slightly nuanced and incredibly subjective. It's a delicate balance between pricing strategies, understanding the market, and understanding your clients' perception of value. But once you master it, the rewards are undoubtedly fruitful. Be patient, keep learning, and don't be afraid to ask for the price you feel your work deserves. Remember, in freelance business, smart pricing is a journey, not a destination.

Chapter 8. Maintaining Stellar Client Relations

Cultivating an excellent relationship with your clients is crucial to any thriving business, more so in the freelance writing world. Nurturing these relationships is a determining factor in the longevity and profitability of your venture. Here's a comprehensive insight into maintaining stellar client relations.

8.1. The Importance of Good Client Relationships

In the realm of freelance writing a sturdy client base is tantamount to having a steady income. As much as maintaining good financial records and delivering top-notch content is critical, so too is nurturing client relationships. Your interaction with clients defines your brand, establishes your professionalism, increases client retention, and broadens your network through referrals. All these, in turn, stabilize and boost your monetary returns.

8.2. Effective Communication

Effective communication forms the backbone of flourishing client relationships. Use simple, clear language and steer clear from complex jargon unless it's necessary. Regularly update your clients on the work progression. This creates trust and confidence in your service. Promptly respond to inquiries, comments, or suggestions. Position yourself as approachable, thus keeping the communication line active and responsive. Strive for clarity, precision, and comprehensiveness in all dialogue.

8.3. Delivering Quality Work

Enhancing your craft continually ensures that you deliver high-quality work. Never compromise on the quality of your output. Read extensively, explore various writing styles, and proofread your work before submissions. Delivering top-tier work endears you to your clients, earning you repeat business and solid referrals.

8.4. Art of Negotiation

Negotiation is an invaluable skill in securing and sustaining client relationships. Understand what your client needs, their budget limits, and be flexible enough to reach common ground. Do not undersell your services, instead find a balance that leaves both you and the client satisfied.

8.5. Maintaining Professionalism

Adhere to set deadlines. Proactivity and time management are hallmarks of professionalism. Manage your work such that you can adjust to sudden changes in project timelines without compromising the stipulated timeline. In cases of unforeseen hiccups, communicate this as early as possible and renegotiate the deadline with your client.

8.6. Handling Difficult Clients

At times, you will encounter challenging clients. Maintain calmness during such situations. Listen keenly to their complaints and respond respectfully. Seek to understand the source of contention and work towards a resolution. Your handling of crisis speaks volumes about your brand and can either make or break your rapport with a client.

8.7. Client Appreciation

Client appreciation goes beyond the formalities of a 'thank you' note. Tailored appreciation forms such as offering discounts on future services, providing extra services at no cost, or occasionally surprising them with tokens goes a long way in maintaining good relations.

8.8. Asking for Reviews and Referrals

Reviews, testimonies, and referrals cement your credibility as a freelance writer. Encourage your clients to leave reviews on your work. Positive reviews improve your market visibilities while criticisms present an opportunity for improvement. With your client's permission, use these testimonies on your website or portfolio. After successfully completing a project, ask for referrals.

In conclusion, prioritizing client relationships is an assured channel of amassing a bountiful income in freelance writing. It requires consistent effort, patience, and resilience. Armed with these strategies, you're set to elevate your freelance writing venture to unmatched heights. Assert your command of words and enjoy the rich rewards of your art.

Chapter 9. Effective Time Management for Freelancers

One of the most critical aspects of running a successful freelance writing business is effective time management. Without this essential skill, you might find yourself overwhelmed by deadlines, unfulfilled personal commitments, and a lack of work-life balance. But don't worry! This section will walk you through the specifics of managing your time as a freelancer.

9.1. The Importance of Time Management

Time is your most precious resource as a freelancer. Juggling multiple projects simultaneously and meeting deadlines is a balancing act that can be made simpler with effective time management. You have the freedom to choose how to spend your time, a rare commodity in today's busy world. This freedom allows you to work at your most productive hours, maximize your earnings, and, if managed well, enjoy ample personal time.

9.2. Proactive vs. Reactive Time Management

Time management can be broadly classified into two types: Proactive and Reactive. Proactive time management emphasizes planning, setting goals, and organizing daily tasks in advance. Contrarily, reactive time management involves dealing with tasks as they come, oftentimes leading to chaos and stress. While a certain level of reactivity is inevitable in freelancing due to unpredictable client demands, strive for a predominantly proactive approach. This way, you can avoid last-minute pressures and provide quality work to your clients.

9.3. Setting Clear Goals

Begin your journey toward effective time management by setting clear and measurable goals. These can be daily, weekly, monthly, or even yearly goals depending on the scope and nature of your freelance writing business. Goals help you maintain focus on critical tasks and provide clarity on how much time to allocate to them.

To set robust goals, consider using the SMART goal framework: Specific, Measurable, Achievable, Relevant, and Time-bound. Ensure your goals adhere to the SMART principles. For example, "I will write 1,000 words for Project A by 10 a.m." is a SMART goal since it precisely mentions what needs to be done within a specific timeframe.

9.4. Prioritizing Your Tasks

Once your goals are in place, the next step is prioritizing. Not all tasks carry equal weight. Understanding this can help you organize your tasks based on importance and urgency.

One method to prioritize tasks is the Eisenhower Matrix, a four-quadrant box that helps you decide on and prioritize tasks by urgency and importance, sorting out less urgent and important tasks that you should either delegate or not do at all. The quadrants are:

1. Important and Urgent: Critical tasks that need immediate attention, such as a project due today.

2. Important, Not Urgent: Tasks like planning, strategizing, and relationship-building, which contribute to long-term success.

3. Not Important, but Urgent: Tasks that demand your attention now but don't contribute significantly to your goals, such as non-

essential emails or calls.

4. Not Important, Not Urgent: Time-wasters that you should avoid or delegate, like unnecessary meetings or non-productive activities.

9.5. Working in Time Blocks

One productivity technique that can significantly enhance your time management is time blocking, or scheduling fixed times each day to work on specific tasks. The Pomodoro Technique, a time-management method developed by Francesco Cirillo, involves breaking your workday into 25-minute chunks separated by five-minute breaks. These intervals are known as "pomodoros." After about four pomodoros, you take a longer break of about 15 to 20 minutes. This method can help keep your mind fresh and focused while working.

9.6. Managing Distractions

In our connected era, distractions are only a click away. Solitude becomes a luxury, especially when you're working from home. Develop strategies to handle common disruptions proactively. These might include turning off social media notifications during work hours, setting boundaries with family members, or working in a dedicated office space at home.

9.7. Establish A Routine

A routine can be a game changer for freelancers. With a fixed pattern, your body and mind adapt to automatically get into 'work mode' during specific hours. Decide on the number of hours you wish to work each day, and divvy them up based on the priority of tasks. It's important to incorporate breaks, relaxation periods, and exercise into your routine to avoid burnout.

9.8. Handing Off Non-Essential Tasks

Sometimes, effective time management means knowing when to delegate. As your freelance business grows, consider hiring a virtual assistant or using automated tools for administrative tasks. This frees up more of your time, allowing you to focus on the core aspect of your business: writing.

Implementing these time management strategies may take time and practice, but soon they'll become second nature, allowing you to sustain a successful freelance writing business. Remember, regardless of the techniques chosen, the aim is to make the best use of your time, striking a balance that works for you.

Chapter 10. The Art of Mastering Consistent Writing

Consistent writing is the cornerstone of a successful freelance writing career. The ability to produce quality content on a regular basis will not only improve your writing skills and discipline, but also heighten your visibility and credibility in the industry. More importantly, it is the fuel that propels your writing business forward. However, mastering this craft isn't a walk in the park—it requires determination, strategic planning, and a lot of practice.

10.1. Establishing a Regular Writing Routine

Creating a consistent writing routine is the first stepping stone to becoming an accomplished freelancer. This is because it shapes your mindset, promoting discipline and focus, which are vital for this endeavor. You must set aside dedicated time for writing each day or week and honor that commitment. It might be two hours every morning, or four hours over the weekend, depending on what works best for you.

There's no one-size-fits-all routine – it's all about personal preference and trial and error. Try different schedules and observe when your creativity flows freely. Are you a morning person, or do you find your creative peak in the small hours? Once you identify your optimal writing hours, stick to them.

10.2. Cultivating a Productive Writing Environment

The environment you write in can significantly impact your

productivity. A cluttered or distraction-filled space might stifle your creativity and hinder your ability to produce consistent results. Therefore, it's essential to create an environment conducive to writing—this might be a dedicated home office, a quiet café, or even a public library.

Ensure the physical comfort of your workspace too. A comfortable chair, good lighting, and a computer setup that doesn't strain your eyes or hands are essential. Avoiding physical discomfort will help keep your focus squarely on your writing.

10.3. Embracing Writing Tools and Software

In today's digital age, numerous tools can simplify your writing process and maintain consistency. Word processing software, grammar and spelling checkers, distraction-free writing tools, and project management applications can all aid in your quest for writing consistency.

Consider utilizing a digital calendar to schedule your writing sessions and track your progress. Tools like Trello can help you manage your projects and deadlines, while grammar checkers like Grammarly can ensure your work is always up to scratch.

10.4. Setting Clear and Achievable Writing Goals

A key aspect of consistent writing is to set clear, measurable, and achievable goals. Forget vague objectives like "I want to write more" and aim for specific targets like "I will write 500 words each day." Having clear goals gives you something to strive for and makes it easier to monitor your progress.

It's important, however, to ensure that these goals are achievable. Setting the bar too high might lead to burnout and frustration. Remember, consistency is about the long game.

10.5. Managing Writing Blocks and Procrastination

Every freelancer encounters the dreaded writer's block and falls victim to procrastination from time to time. The trick is to not let these challenges stunt your progress. Instead, find effective strategies to overcome them.

For writer's block, try changing your environment, doing some freewriting exercises, or taking a short break. For procrastination, understand your triggers—do you put off writing because you're not in the right mood or because the task seems too daunting? Whatever the reason, knowing why you procrastinate could be the first step in overcoming it.

10.6. Making Writing a Priority

Finally, make writing a priority. It's deceptively easy to put off writing for other tasks, especially when freelance writing gives you the freedom to dictate your own schedule. But given its integral role in your freelance career, writing should arguably be the first item on your daily agenda, not the last.

Without consistent writing, your progress as a freelancer will always be sporadic and unbalanced. But with it, you'll see gradual improvement, a steady stream of work, and ultimately, the thriving freelance business you've dreamed of. It's a demanding craft and discipline—not everyone has the luxury and courage to create and share pieces of their mind. But once you master it, there's no stopping you from reaching the zenith of success in the freelance writing universe.

Remember, every word, every sentence, every paragraph you put down is a step forward in this writing journey. So, keep writing, be consistent, and watch as the opportunities unfold in front of you.

Chapter 11. Exploring Multiple Income Streams in Freelance Writing

Freelance writing can be an adventure, more so when you explore multiple revenue streams. When you break out of the single-source income approach and start developing multiple income streams, not only does your earning potential increase, but you also find the financial stability and flexibility that is quintessential to a structure-free lifestyle like freelancing.

11.1. The concept of multiple income sources

Reality check, no freelance writing job is secure. Clients can come and go, the market can fluctuate, and a myriad of unanticipated events can quite literally dry up your single stream of income. Building several income streams is the ideal way to buffer against such uncertainties. The aim is to avoid putting all your eggs in one basket. Broadly diversifying your capabilities and spreading them across different avenues can help sustainable revenue flow.

By adopting this multifaceted income approach, you help shield your business from the upsets of losing a major client or any slowdown. Additionally, this business model also offers the opportunity for growth and higher earnings. Remember the age-old adage 'do not put all your eggs in one basket'? Here's where it applies splendidly.

11.2. Starting multiple income streams

Some may argue about the potential pitfalls of juggling multiple projects or say that it's more comfortable focusing on one type of writing. We advocate balance. Don't scatter so thin that efficiency drops, but don't restrict so much that you stagnate. The key lies in selecting a few, carefully chosen, assorted income streams that match your interests, skills, and schedule.

Here are some avenues you may want to consider:

1. Creating a blog and monetizing it

2. Article and content writing for websites

3. Ghostwriting: biographies, blogs, books

4. Technical writing

5. Sales copy, marketing content, press releases

6. Ebooks, self publishing

7. Writing courses, coaching, workshops

8. Affiliate marketing

Remember to weigh the pros and cons before venturing onto any path. Exploring multiple income streams does not mean adding everything indiscriminately. It means adding strategic income sources that can work together to build a more substantial, more reliable freelance writing business.

11.3. Monetizing a blog

Blogging can be a lucrative component of your multiple income streams. By creating a blog around a specific subject or niche, you can attract an audience and pave the way for monetization. Here are some ways you can profit:

1. Ads: Websites like Google AdSense can pay to put their ads on your site.

2. Sponsored posts: Companies may pay you to write a post related to their product or service.

3. Affiliate Marketing: By promoting other's products and earning a commission on any sales made through your referral.

Remember, your blog should be a reflection of your unique voice and perspective, so make it original, informative, and engaging. In the world of blogging, content is king, and consistency is queen.

11.4. Content Writing, Ghostwriting, and Technical Writing

Content Writing, Ghostwriting, and Technical Writing are three vital facets of the freelance writing world. Content writing involves creating articles and blog posts for companies to boost their online presence. Ghostwriting, on the other hand, is writing under someone else's name. High-profile people often hire ghostwriters for their biographies, blogs, and even social media posts.

Technical writing requires specialized knowledge as you may be tasked to create manuals, user guides, documentation for software/Hardware products, etc. While these areas might require specific skills and knowledge, they can be highly profitable if you have the knack for them.

11.5. Writing Ebooks and Self Publishing

With the advent of the digital age, self-publishing an ebook has never been easier. It allows you to establish authority in your chosen field and create a passive income stream. You write the ebook once but continue earning with each sale.

11.6. Conducting Writing Courses, Coaching, and Workshops

If you have some experience under your belt, why not pass on your knowledge? Conducting workshops or creating an online course can not only earn you income but also raise your profile as an expert in the field. With online platforms like Udemy or Coursera, you can reach a global audience.

11.7. The Final Thought

Establishing multiple income streams as a freelance writer requires patience and determination. However, the rewards can be significantly satisfying and far-reaching both in terms of personal satisfaction and financial gain.

Remember, you control your freelance writing destiny. Start small, stay consistent, and soon you'll watch your multiple income streams flow into a powerful river of steady revenue. No matter what streams you select, remember that success ultimately lies in providing value with your words, meeting deadlines, and exceeding customer expectations.